Selected Poems
by Sylvia Plath

A Study Guide by Ray Moore

Acknowledgements:

Thanks, as always, are due to Barbara for reading the manuscript and making many helpful suggestions, and for putting the text into the correct formats for publication. Any errors which remain are my own.

I am indebted to the work of numerous translators, biographers, and critics as I have acknowledged in the Bibliography. As always, I am very aware that I stand on the shoulders of giants. Where I am conscious of having taken an idea, or actual words, from a particular author, I have cited the source in the text. Any failure to do so is an omission which I will immediately correct if it is drawn to my attention.

Where I have selectively quoted from the writings of others in the course of my own argument, I have done so in the sincere belief that this constitutes fair use.

Contents

Sylvia Plath: Biographical Fact file

Born: 27th October, 1932 in Boston, Massachusetts, U.S.A.

Father: Otto Emil Plath (who had emigrated to America from Grabowa, Poland, at the age of 15 years), Professor at Boston University.

Mother: Aurelia Schober, a first-generation American of Austrian descent.

Raised: Winthrop, Massachusetts, a town on the Atlantic coast. Plath's early years were dominated by her love of the sea and the coast.

Death of father: Otto Plath died after a long illness in November 1940 when Plath was only nine years old. Ted Hughes (later her husband) writes that she "worshipped her father." When she was first told of his death, she said immediately, "I'll never speak to God again." On the day of her father's death, Plath wrote out a note and made her mother sign it. The note read, "I promise never to marry again." Strangely, she also insisted on going to school and behaving as if nothing had happened.

Education: Plath was an outstanding student who developed a love of Literature. In September 1950, she entered Smith College where she studied hard and began writing short stories, two of which were printed. As her family was not financially well off, Plath depended on scholarships throughout her university education and was never entirely free of financial anxiety.

First suicide attempt: In the summer of 1953, following several weeks of intense depression Plath swallowed a large number of sleeping pills before hiding in the cellar of the house. She was found by her brother three days later very ill but alive. She was admitted to hospital and subsequently underwent electro-convulsive therapy. By the mid-winter of the same year she was able to return to Smith from which in 1955 she graduated summa cum laude.

Education: Between 1955 and 1957, Plath studied on a Fulbright scholarship at Newnham College, Cambridge, and continued to develop her own creative writing.

Marriage: February 1956 Plath met, and almost immediately fell in love with, Ted Hughes, also a student at Cambridge and already a poet of growing reputation. In June, they were married secretly because Plath feared the loss of her Fulbright scholarship if she was no longer single. On 1st April, 1960, Plath gave birth to Frieda Rebecca; in February 1961, she suffered a miscarriage; and in January 1962, Nicholas Farrar was born. The marriage became increasingly strained and there was talk of a separation. This eventually happened in September 1962. [Tragically, Nicholas Hughes committed suicide on Monday,

March 16, 2009 at his home in Alaska following a long struggle against depression.]

Death: 11th February 1963, Sylvia Plath was found unconscious with her head in the gas oven. She had left a note in which she gave her doctor's telephone number and asked anyone finding her to call him. The baby-sitter was expected at 9 a.m. and she came on time, but she was unable to get into Plath's flat for some time. Plath was pronounced dead on arrival at University College Hospital.

Published work: Plath's first book of poems, *The Colossus*, was published in 1960 and her novel *The Bell Jar* in 1963, but most of Sylvia Plath's poetry was published after her death. *Ariel*, a collection of her later poems which contains "Daddy" was published in 1965.

Sigmund Freud (1856-1939) the founder of psychoanalysis.

Freud's theories on the developing sexuality of young males and females help the reader to understand Sylvia Plath's poem "Daddy". Plath had certainly read and been influenced by Freud's theories.

It should be stressed that there is a difference between understanding Freud's theories and believing them. Indeed, Freud himself was continually changing his theories as his understanding of the human mind developed.

Freud argued that for all babies, regardless of their sex, the first human to excite feeling of love is the mother since it is the mother who provides food, warmth and physical comfort. As the baby becomes an infant, however, marked differences develop between the sexes. The boy infant typically deepens his attachment to the mother whilst increasingly coming to regard the father as a rival for the love and attention of the mother. The girl infant is typically attracted to the father and comes to see the mother as a rival.

As the boy-child enters adolescence, the attraction to the mother weakens. There may be many factors for this change: the boy is more aware of the mother's age in relation to his own youth; he becomes aware that certain kinds of feelings for his mother are not acceptable to society; the mother constantly fails to live up to his ideal of her; he finds a more appropriate object for his feelings of love in a girl of his own age.

In girls, the process is similar, although the girl's attraction to the father is often stronger and more enduring than is the boy's to the mother. The same factors, however, tend to weaken the tie.

It must be stressed that these phases (called by Freud the Oedipus Complex and the Electra Complex respectively) occur in all of us and are therefore quite normal and healthy. Problems occur only when an individual fails to progress satisfactorily through the stages and into adulthood. A mature man who has never developed out of the stage of being attracted to his mother, or a woman who retains her sexual attraction to her father, may repress this feeling (because they know how horrible society feel it to be) and this may result in serious psychological problems.

Guide to the Selected Poems of Sylvia Plath

How to Use this Study Guide:

The aim of this Guide is to help you towards a fuller understanding and appreciation of the poems of Sylvia Plath. For each poem in the collection the Guide provides a brief introduction and a number of questions. Some questions are carefully worded to draw your attention to important aspects of the poem which you need to understand. Other questions are very open-ended: they are not designed to lead you in any direction, but simply to ask for your ideas. It should always be clear to you which type of question you are being asked. Although they can be used in a variety of ways, the questions work best as an aid to small group discussion.

Literary terms are in ***bold italics***. These terms are defined towards the end of this guide. An activity is also included to aid in the understanding of these terms.

Plath's poems do not unfold their meaning to a superficial reading. She demands a lot of her readers, but the rewards are usually worth the effort.

MISS DRAKE PROCEEDS TO SUPPER

The setting of this poem is a hospital ward. Plath is drawing on her experience of women's wards which she gained during her pregnancies and her operation for appendicitis. The poem is a *comic* description of the extravagant care with which Miss Drake walks to the dining room.

1. Give and briefly explain examples of humor in the description of Miss Drake's progress.

SPINSTER

A sad little tale in which we can see Plath's reverence for love and life and her hatred of life-denying isolation.

Verses 1 - 2

1. What emotion is it which the girl suddenly feels and why does she dislike it so violently?

2. Collect together the words and phrases which suggest the lack of order in the world.

Explain any that need explanation.

Verse 3

3. What characteristics of winter appear attractive to the girl? How are they described?

Verses 4 - 5

4. Which words and phrases suggest how threatening the girl found the emotion released by her walk with her "latest suitor"?

5. What is so sad about the last line of the poem?

MAUDLIN

This is a very difficult poem. The following ideas are offered tentatively.

1. "Maudlin" means foolishly tearful or sentimental. The word is derived from the Middle English "Maudelen" a spelling of the name Mary Magdalene, the woman taken in adultery and saved from stoning by Christ, who is typically portrayed as a tearful penitent.

2. The first verse has several references to the woman's menstrual cycle. This is related to the movements of the moon which is here male (as in the man in the moon).

3. The male (*symbolized* by "faggot-bearing Jack" is certainly described in a critical way as arrogant, lacking in feeling, perhaps drunken.

4. As mermaids, women have no need of men (another reflection of the *theme* of self-sufficiency in Plath), but they give this up at great cost to be able to have sex with men. Read in this way, the poem seems a complete counter-argument to the previous poem.

RESOLVE

For the most part, this poem offers a simple but evocative description of an ordinary day in a misty, cold autumn.

1. Much of the description is purely realistic and gives the impression of having been directly observed (e.g., "the one-eared cat / laps its gray paw," "a milk-film blurs / the empty bottles on the windowsill"). These are, however, details of the description which appear to have a *symbolic* dimension suggesting a religious significance to the poem. Can you locate these details?

2. Who do you take the "twelve black-gowned examiners" to be?

3. Explain the significance of the title of the poem.

NIGHT SHIFT

The speaker describes her initial shock at hearing the repeated beating in the night – a shock not shared by her neighbors who are accustomed to it.

1. What is meant by the line, "It took root at my coming"?

2. Once she has discovered the cause, how does the speaker seem to feel about the noise?

3. Why do you think that the speaker repeats the phrase, "tending, without stop"?

4. Which of Plath's other poems embody a similar attitude to the effect on humanity of industrialization?

FULL FATHOM FIVE

The title of this poem is taken from the opening lines of Shakespeare's *The Tempest:*

> Full fathom five thy father lies
> Of his bones are coral made.

The *theme* of the poem is Plath's dead father and the sea is equated with death.

1. It is clear that the old man seldom surfaces, but what does the description make clear about those times when he does so?

2. What dangers are involved for the speaker in the surfacing of the father?

3. Look closely at the final verse. Does it indicate that the speaker has chosen a line of action?

SUICIDE OFF EGG ROCK

Egg Rock is in the public domain.

The poem describes a suicide against an unattractive industrial background. (Ochre is a yellow/orange color. A comber is a long, curling wave.) You can find photographs of Egg Rock on the Internet.

1. The opening sentence describes what was behind and what in front of the man as he stood on the edge of the water contemplating suicide. How is this setting made unattractive?

2. In the remainder of verse 1, how does the poem point the contrast between the man and the other people on the sand?

3. Verse 2 describes the man standing on the beach at the edge of the water contemplating suicide. How does the verse make it clear that the man regards both his life and the alternative of death as horrific?

4. In the final four lines, Egg Rock seems to be given an importance which suggests a *symbolic* meaning. Can you suggest what it might *symbolize*?

5. The man finally walks into the water to die. Is this presented in the poem as positive or negative and how do you know?

THE HERMIT AT OUTERMOST HOUSE

Plath's early poems show several examples of strong, defiant, unmovable male figures, and the hermit is one of these.

1. How does verse 1 establish the hermit's indestructibility?

2. At what is the hermit laughing on his doorstep?

3.   The last three verses of the poem try to establish in what lay the hermit's superiority to the "Hard gods". The clue seems to lie in the **symbolic** significance of "a certain meaning green". What connotations does the color green have?

MEDALLION

The speaker recalls finding a dead snake. The poem is full of precisely observed detail.

1. How was the snake killed?

2. What parts of the description suggest the beauty of the snake?

3. How does the speaker bring home the fact of the snake's death?

4.   What do you make of the **image**, "Knifelike he was chaste enough, / Pure death's-metal..."

THE MANOR GARDEN

Written in the late autumn of 1959 when Plath was pregnant with her first child. These two facts may be of great help in understanding this poem.

1. What season is described in verse one? How do you know?

2. Who is the "You" addressed in verses 1, 2 and 3?

3. What do you make of the final verse? Can you find any suggestion of hope in the last two lines?

THE STONES

The speaker is a patient in hospital (the "city" of the first line), but her attitude to the healing process which she is undergoing is deeply ambiguous.

1. Which words, phrases and *images* suggest to you the speaker's feeling of helplessness as a patient?

2. Which words, phrases and *images* suggest to you the speaker's feeling that as a patient she is the victim of violence?

3. How optimistic do you find the final line of the poem?

THE BURNT-OUT SPA

The poem describes a building destroyed by fire in contrast to the stream which flows past unchanged. (A "spa" is a place where a mineral spring is found. A "dell" is a small wooded hollow. "Karakul" is a type of wool. "Ichor" in Greek myth is the fluid said to flow in the veins of the Gods, but in modern pathology it is a foul-smelling watery discharge from a wound or ulcer.)

1. The first five verses are an ***extended personification*** of the destroyed building as a dead man. Trace the stages of this ***image.***

2. Explain the line, "The small dell eats what ate it once."

3. Why do you think that the speaker is so firm in rejecting the idea that the woman she sees reflected in the stream "is not I"? Who are "the durable ones"?

4. Why do you think that the speaker concludes, "The stream that hustles us / Neither nourished nor heals"?

YOU'RE

Written during Plath's first pregnancy, this poem is a string of loving, humorous, absurd descriptions of the baby which the speaker is carrying.

1. What is being described in the first two and a half lines?

2. What happened to the dodo? Why does the unborn baby give a "thumbs-down on the Dodo's mode"?

3. What other ***images*** are used to describe the unborn baby in verses 1 and 2? Which is your favorite and why?

FACE LIFT

Plath's friend Dido Merwin has a cosmetic operation which inspired this poem. What attracts Plath to the subject is the **theme** of rebirth which it allows her to explore.

1. How is the voice of the poem different in the first three lines as compared with the rest of the poem?

2. Why is the **image** of "mummy-cloths" particularly well chosen given the **themes** of the poem?

3. How is the speaker's first experience of anesthetic made unattractive?

4. How is the speaker's more recent experience of anesthetic made to appear pleasant?

5. Explain the **image** in the line, "Tapped like a cask, the years draining into my pillow."

6. Why is the poodle "dead"?

7. How does the speaker now regard the older self whom she has cast off? (Examine particularly the section, "Now she's done for ... her thin hair.")

8. In what sense is the speaker "mother to myself"?

MORNING SONG

A delightfully simple poem celebrating the life of the speaker's child written after the birth of Plath's own daughter.

1. In what ways is the **image** in the opening line appropriate to describe the origin of a Baby's life?

2. What does the speaker mean by 'your nakedness shadows our safety'?

3. Try to explain the **image** in verse 3.

4. How appropriate are the animal **images** in verse 5?

5. What is the effect of the **image** on the last line of the poem?

TULIPS

Written 18th March, 1961, this is a poem based on the experience of being a patient in a hospital where time seems to have another meaning and extremes of feeling are dulled by the daily routine. The speaker has given herself up to the doctors; her fate is entirely in their hands. In the hospital world of whiteness and motionlessness, the red tulips sent by her husband are an intrusion, **symbols** of the life of activity outside. Like the photographs of her husband and children, the flowers disturb her, trying to pull her back to her normal life, away from the peace of the hospital.

Verses 1 - 3

1. Although the speaker seems to be enjoying the "peacefulness" which she has learned, certain words, phrases and **images** draw the reader's attention to the inherent dangers of such a way of life. Make a list of these and add comments as necessary.

2. What two kinds of "baggage" does the speaker reject in verse 3?

Verses 4 - 6

3. What **images** are used in verse 4 to describe the process by which the speaker has been stripped of all of the different aspects of her life? What is the significance of the **image** of drowning which is used?

4. Once again, in verse 5 an approving description by the speaker is actually given rather ominous overtones by the poet. Where?

5. Why are the tulips like a "baby"? Why does the speaker think of them as like an "awful Baby"?

6. Explain, "Their redness talks to my wound, it corresponds."

7. The last three lines of verse 6 return to the **image** of drowning. Comment on this in the light of the previous drowning **image**.

Verses 7 - 9

8. In verse 7 the tulips finally force the speaker to review the state into which she has fallen under the influence of the hospital. What change of attitude is clear?

9. By the end of the poem, what effect have the tulips had upon the speaker?

INSOMNIAC

1. What *image* is used to describe the night sky?

2. What *image* is used to describe sleeplessness?

3. In verse 2 the poem describes the waking thoughts of the insomniac. What is their nature and what *images* are used to describe them?

4. What does the poem mean by describing the experience which the sleeping pills used to give the insomniac as, "A life baptized in no-like for a while"?

5. The final verse contains two extended *images* of the man's suffering. What do you think they mean?

WUTHERING HEIGHTS

The title of this poem suggests that the speaker is walking on the bleak and cold Yorkshire moors up to the ruined farmhouse which is the setting for Emily Bronte's novel of the same name. (In reality, the house is called Top Withens.)

Eileen Aird defines the *theme* of the poem in this way, "the vast expanses of uncivilized nature are... seen as more powerful than all the fortifications of structured society."

Brita Lindberg-Seyersted writes, "The solitary wanderer bravely 'step[s] forward,' but nature is her enemy: the alluring horizons 'dissolve' at her advance, wind and heather try to undo her. *Images* of landscape and animals are consistently turned into *metaphors* for the human intruder's feeling of being insignificant and exposed.

Verse one:

1. The *simile* "ring me like faggots" compares the speaker to a witch being burned for heresy. This immediately tells us a lot about how the speaker is feeling about herself. Make a list of words and phrases which come to mind.

2. Actually, Plath was not alone when she visited Wuthering Heights – she was with her husband Ted Hughes. How does that information add to the impression you have of the speaker?

3. This verse describes an experience which everyone who has walked in hilly country will recall. What happens to the seemingly firm lines of the horizon as you walk on? How is this described in the poem? Comment particularly on the *simile* "dissolve / Like a series of promises."

4. The one positive in the entire verse is the hope that "Touched by a match, they [the faggots] might warm me," and that the lighted faggots might 'pin' the constantly-moving horizon. Lighting the faggots would, of course, be a human action. It would prove that the speaker was not alone in the world. On the other hand...?

Verse two:

5. The speaker stresses how out of place she is in this environment. The enemy of life is the cold wind. Which lines imply that the wind is deliberately attacking the speaker? Why is this?

Verse three:

6. The speaker is intimidated by the sheep because (unlike her) they are at home in this environment. When the sheep look at her directly, she writes, "It is like being mailed into space, / A thin, silly message." What is she feeling? Why

7. The sheep are said to "stand about in grandmotherly disguise, / All wig curls and yellow teeth." This is a reference to the disguise used in Little Red Riding Hood. What does the reference to this fairy tale add to the picture you are building of the speaker's psychological condition?

Verse four:

8. The speaker comes to an abandoned and ruined building. What is left and what is not left of the farmhouse at Wuthering Heights? Why does the speaker find this so threatening?

9. The end of the verse perhaps contains a reference to the novel *Wuthering Heights* in which the spirit of Cathy cries out to be readmitted to the house. Now, however, the only sound of the wind is "a few odd syllables. / It rehearses them moaningly: / Black stone, black stone." What connotations do the last four words carry for you?

Verse five:

10. What comparison is suggested by the ***metaphor***, "The grass is beating its head distractedly"?

11. The poem ends with a ***paradox***, "Now, in valleys narrow / And black as purses, the house lights / Gleam like small change." The only light (and by implication warmth) lies where? But the light turns out to be only "small change." What does this add to your understanding of what the speaker feels about herself in relation to society?

FINISTERRE

Cape Finisterre is a headland in NW Spain, the westernmost point of the Spanish mainland. On the evidence of the poem, there is a statue there dedicated to sailors lost at sea.

I have no way of knowing whether Plath had the following passage from "Place-Names: The Name: (which is the final section of *Swann's Way*, the first book of Proust's *Remembrance of Things Past*), but it makes a great introduction to this poem:

> 'You feel there [Balbec], below your feet still ... far more even than at Finistère ... you feel that you are actually at the land's end of France, of Europe, of the Old World. And it is the ultimate encampment of the fishermen, precisely like the fishermen who have lived since the world's beginning, facing the everlasting kingdom of the sea-fogs and shadows of the night.' ... I tried to form a picture in my mind of how those fishermen had lived, the timid and unsuspecting essay towards social intercourse which they had attempted there, clustered upon a promontory of the shores of hell, at the foot of the cliffs of death.

1. Verse 1 describes the sea and the cliffs. Is this presented as a place of beauty?

2. Why are the "trefoils" (small flowers) said to be "close to death"?

3. In the last two lines of verse 2, how does the speaker describe the experience of walking in the mists generated by the waves crashing against the rocks?

4. To the speaker, the statue of Our Lady appears to have taken on a significance different from that intended by its builders. Can you explain?

5. Verse 4 describes the inevitable tourist traps - the stalls which sell trinkets and food.

6. How do the final lines of direct speech reflect the **themes** of the poem?

THE MOON AND THE YEW TREE

A poem dated 22nd October, 1961. I find this a very difficult poem. Perhaps the best thing that I can do is to offer the following tentative interpretation for your criticism: The dominant impression is the speaker's feeling that she is trapped and that she "cannot see where there is to get to." The speaker lives in the "planetary" world: the yew tree represents the male principle ("cold," "black," "silent," "deathly"); the moon represents the female principle ("bald and wild", "terribly upset" and in "complete despair"). A possible escape route is offered by the Church "affirming the Resurrection," that is, hope of life in triumph over the despair of death. How desperately the speaker would like "to believe in tenderness," but she cannot. What happens in the Church has no impact upon either the moon or the yew tree: theirs is the terrible reality offering no hope of salvation.

MIRROR

A reasonably straightforward poem cast rather in the form of a medieval riddle, except that the title supplies the solution!

1. In verse 1, how does the voice in the poem seek to establish the objectivity of the *image* that the mirror gives?

2. The woman searches "for what she really is". Why does the speaker regard "the candles or the moon" as "liars"? Is the speaker right to do so?

3. Explain the *image* in the last two lines.

THE BABYSITTERS

Dated 29th October, 1961. The main *theme* of this poem is Time: Time the inevitable destroyer of a happiness which, before it was lost, we simply took for granted and so didn't even think of as happiness.

1. How are these ideas developed in the poem?

LITTLE FUGUE

Written in 1962, this must be one of Plath's most difficult poems, so I suggest that you leave it until you have read all of the other poems in the book. The **themes** explored are very similar to those in "Daddy" though that poem has a clarity which this poem does not have. The poem follows the speaker's stream of consciousness as she makes connections which are personally meaningful but not immediately clear to the reader. As with much of Plath's poetry, we sense that the writing is heavily **symbolic** but the **symbolism** is also deeply personal and therefore hard to 'unlock.' I am going to offer a tentative reading of the poem on which I hope you will be able to build. The word 'fugue' has a number of meanings. Perhaps the most relevant to this poem is "a pathological disturbance of consciousness" (Webster's dictionary). The poem's subject is Plath's father, or rather her failure to communicate with him in death as in life, and her attempt to come to terms with his death by opening up communications with the dead and (ultimately) by wishing to join the dead.

The poem opens with opposites: the black of the "deaf and dumb" yew tree and the white of the "blind" clouds, representing respectively the realms the living and of the dead, and the absolute failure of communication between the two. Yet the blind pianist managed to "hear Beethoven" and somehow managed to communicate with the death by brings the two realms together in the form of the black and white keys of the piano. That is why the speaker "couldn't stop looking" because she cannot make this kind of contact. The Grosse Fugue (composed in 1824 by Beethoven who was by that time becoming profoundly deaf) is a "yew hedge" presumably because of its technical difficulty. The speaker envies "big noises" because since her father's death she has been left only with silence. She figuratively describes herself as a deaf person with a "dark funnel" (an ear trumpet) desperately trying to hear her dead father. She is thus led specifically to childhood memories of her father, "A yew hedge of orders, / Gothic and barbarous, pure German. / Dead men cry from it. / I am guilty of nothing." These lines describe her father figuratively as a German soldier in World War II, a soldier who was guilty of the massacre of Jews. The speaker claims to be, like the Jews, an innocent victim. She associates herself with the yew tree and the yew tree with Christ, for both suffered on earth to redeem the dead. The father is next described figuratively as a butcher, "Lopping off the sausages!" in a California delicatessen during World War I. (Of course, Plath's father was a scientist with a Ph.D.) This is another **image** of the Holocaust. The silence "of another order" is caused by the death of the father leaving her with only a "lame ... memory" of a Prussian man with one leg (Plath's father had a leg amputated because of diabetes). The speaker feels that death had opened to her once and may again, "Now similar clouds / Are spreading their vacuous sheets." As death once came for her father, the speaker senses that it is about to come for her. However, in the final stanza she presents herself as a survivor, "I survive the while, / Arranging my morning. / These are my fingers, this my baby. / The clouds are a marriage of dress, of that pallor." She takes refuge in the conventional roles of wife and mother, but almost everything in the verse has ominous undertones, for example, the **pun** on "morning"/mourning, the marriage is merely one of "dress," and the "pallor" suggests the whiteness of a shroud.

1. Several of Plath's poems use World War II Holocaust *imagery* to describe her feelings about the father she lost at the age of eight. She identifies herself, and the suffering she experienced as a result of her personal loss, with that of the Jews persecuted by the Nazis. This has proved unacceptable to many readers and critics. Susan Gubar, for example, says categorically, "Plath's non-Jewishness as well as her lack of a personal stake in the disaster made her speaking on behalf of the victims appear [to be] a desecration." Where do you stand on this issue of Plath appropriating *images* from mass slaughter to describe her own feelings of loss, victimization, anger, etc.?

2. The poem is full of *puns* (starting with yew / you), some of which are darkly *comic*. Find as many examples as you can.

3. How do you feel about poems which are so difficult to understand? (I actually find some of the literary criticism on this poem completely obscure!)

CROSSING THE WATER

The title indicates that this is a poem of transition, but the *symbols* defy a simple meaning. The most obvious connotation of crossing the water is of dead souls crossing the River Styx that in Greek mythology separates the world of the living from the world of the dead.

1. What do you understand by the *image* "cut-paper people"?

2. The *image* of the pale hand rising out of the water recalls the hand which rose out of the lake to take back Arthur's sword following his final defeat. What threat does the "snag" pose to those crossing the water?

3. In classical myth, the Sirens called sailors to destruction on rocks. Who are the sirens in this poem and what is their dangerous message?

4. What do you make of the final line, and, in particular, of the word "This"?

AMONG THE NARCISSI

This poem has few difficulties. In it Plath shows her admiration for the power of the life-force.

1. What similarities do you find between Percy and the man described in "The Hermit at Outermost House"?

POPPIES IN JULY

Written in the summer of 1962 when her marriage to Ted Hughes was breaking up. The *theme* of the poem is the speaker's inability to be touched by the Poppies: she can neither feel the pain of their flames not can she enjoy the dulling sleep of their opiate.

1. Why do you think that it exhausts the speaker to watch the poppies?

2. What two *images* are used to describe the petals of the poppies?

3. What do you think is meant by "this glass capsule"?

4. What do you make of the last line?

THE BEE MEETING

In June 1962, Plath and Hughes became, like many of the villagers, beekeepers. This poem is largely descriptive, and these aspects present little difficulty. The incident, however, becomes *symbolic* of the speaker's fear at once of being isolated and of being assimilated into the group with the loss of her identity.

1. Explain the process by which the speaker becomes assimilated into the group of villagers and indistinguishable from them.

2. What is it that the villagers are doing to the hive and why should the old queen be grateful?

3. Why is the speaker so cold at the end of the poem?

Selected Poems by Sylvia Plath

DADDY

Written 12th October 1962, this is one of Plath's most obviously autobiographical poems in that many details of the life of the speaker are identical to those of Plath. The reader should, however, be cautious about assuming that the speaker is simply Plath.

1. Having read the poem a number of times, write a paragraph giving your initial reactions and your first impressions of its meaning. Share your initial impressions, discuss them and write a paragraph on what you have learned from this sharing.

2. There are a number of references in the poem to the role of Germany in World War II (e.g., "Dachau ... Luftwaffe ... Aryan ... Fascist" etc.) and to Vampirism and the Occult ("Taroc ... a stake in your ... heart" etc.). Find as many of these types of references as you can and by discussion and research try to understand them. Give an account of how your efforts to understand the meaning of these references. What became clearer about the meaning of the poem and what remains obscure?

3. Read and discuss the sheet on Freud. What light does it shed on the poem? Construct two parallel timelines, one for the life of Sylvia Plath and the other for the woman who is speaking in the poem. Mark off the significant events for each. Highlight any differences.

4. You should now be in a position to explain the *theme* of the poem and to explore at least some of the ways in which this *theme* is developed (e.g., the significance of the references to World War II and to Vampirism and the Occult should be clear by now).

5. Much of the poem is devoted to expressing the speaker's feelings about her father. This is done in a series of *images*, mainly *metaphors* (e.g., "black shoe," "a bag full of God," etc.).

Make a complete list of these *images* and discuss what feelings they suggest.

6. Listen to Sylvia Plath reading this poem. What does her reading of the poem add to your understanding of it and your feelings about it?

7. Read the work of a range of critics on the poem. With what did you agree/disagree?

Activity: Keeping a Reading Diary of "Daddy" by Sylvia Plath.

A normal diary is used to record a person's thoughts, feelings and experiences each day in the context of important events in her/his life. A reading diary follows the same principle, but this time the context is provided by the person's experiences of a text.

In the case of a novel, a reading diary might include separate entries for each chapter, recording the reader's developing thoughts, feelings and experiences as the novel gradually unfolds. With a short text such as "Daddy", this sort of approach is clearly not possible. "Daddy" is, however, a complex poem which is not to be understood fully at a first, second, or even a third reading. Your diary entries will be made at various stages in your reading and re-reading of the poem. In this way, the diary should form a record of your developing understanding (and, I hope, appreciation) of this remarkable piece of writing.

You should include any of the following in your diary entries: impressions and emotional responses (particularly in your early readings, the poem may produce strong feelings and these should be explored, even if you don't quite understand why or how they are produced); guesses at what the poem, or parts of it, may be saying (present your guesses as just that - hypotheses to be tested by later re-reading - and don't worry about offering alternative guesses particularly in the early entries); questions about parts that you don't understand (be honest and try to define exactly what it is that is causing you problems and how you might go about finding solutions); an account of any research or activity which you have done and how these have helped you to understand the poem (always come back to the poem, to the words on the page and your relationship to them); and your frustrations/anger/joy/excitement/ etc. (say what you really feel about this piece of writing). This list is intended to open up possibilities for you and not to restrict them. If you can think of other types of entry then please use them.

As your diary progresses, you will change your mind. Earlier statements will appear to be wrong, perhaps embarrassingly so! This does not matter at all! What does matter is that the diary shows you progressing towards a mature understanding of the poem, remembering always that in any work of literature there is some room for different interpretations and for widely different valuations of the quality of the text as a piece of writing.

Selected Poems by Sylvia Plath

It is important that you stick to the following structure:

Activity One:
The poem will be read aloud by the teacher and you will be given some time to re-read it.

ENTRY ONE: Write a paragraph giving your initial reaction to the poem and your first impressions of its meaning.

Activity Two:
In a small group share your initial impressions and discuss them.

ENTRY TWO: Write a paragraph on what you have learned from this sharing.

Activity Three:
There are a number of references in the poem to the role of Germany in World War II (e.g., Dachau, Luftwaffe, Aryan, Fascist, etc.), to Vampirism and the Occult

("Taroc ... a stake in your ... heart," etc.). In a group, find as many of these types of references as you can and by discussion and research try to understand them.

ENTRY THREE: In a longer entry, give an account of how your efforts to understand the meaning of these references. What became clearer about the meaning of the poem and what remained obscure? What use does the writer appear to be making of these references?

Activity Four:
Read and in groups discuss the sheet on Freud. What light does it shed on the poem? Construct two parallel timelines, one for the life of Sylvia Plath and the other for the person who is speaking in the poem. Mark off the significant events for each.

ENTRY FOUR: You should now be in a position to explain the *theme* of the poem and explore at least some of the ways in which this *theme* is developed (e.g., the significance of the references to World War II and to Vampirism and the Occult should be clear by now).

Activity Five:
Much of the poem is devoted to expressing the speaker's feelings about her father. This is done in a series of *images*, mainly *metaphors* (e.g., "black shoe ...a bag full of God," etc.). In groups, make a complete list of these *images* and discuss what feelings they suggest.

ENTRY FIVE: Write about the use of *imagery* in the poem to describe the father.

Activity Six:

Go through the poem and isolate any words, lines or sections which still do not make sense to you. Work in a group to sort out the meaning and as a last, desperate, measure, ask the teacher.

ENTRY SIX: You should now be able to give your considered understanding of the poem. Avoid repeating in detail points which you have already covered by referring back to them.

Keep in mind these three questions: What is the writer saying? How is she saying it? How effective is what she has written?

Activity Seven:

Listen to Sylvia Plath reading this poem.

ENTRY SEVEN: What does her reading of the poem add to your understanding of it and your feelings about it?

Activity Eight:

Read a critical essay on the poem.

ENTRY EIGHT: What did you agree with/disagree with?

LESBOS

Lesbos is a Greek island which gives its name to Lesbianism. (If you don't know why, find out.) The basic situation seems to be this: the speaker has two young children but there is no reference to a father. The speaker's friend has one child and a husband who appear to be unfaithful and unable to satisfy her sexually. The friend is trying to dominate the speaker who finally rejects her. If this overview is accurate, it should help you to understand some of the details of the poem.

CUT

The poem begins with a simple and graphic description of something we've all probably either done or come close to doing - slicing the top off of a finger whilst cutting vegetables. The remaining flesh at the top of the finger is compared to a hat and the blood running from the cut to the loose folds of skin in a turkey's neck.

BY CANDLELIGHT

Written 24th October, 1962, after Hughes had left but before she had moved from the cottage in Dorset. The poem has obvious similarities with "Nick and the Candlestick."

1. Describe the setting of the poem as it is given in stanza one. (Start with an old cottage in the country without electricity.)

2. The "fluid" in which the speaker and her baby meet is the fluctuating light on the candle. What does this light/fluid **symbolize**? (Think of *Macbeth*, "Out, out, brief candle! Life's but a walking shadow, a poor player that struts and frets his hour upon the stage and is heard no more. It is a tale told by an idiot, full of sound and fury, signifying nothing.")

3. Stanzas three and four describe the birth of the speaker's baby. What do you find important about the way that coming to life is described?

4. The "brass man" is Atlas - the candlestick is made in the form of Atlas holding up the candle. In mythology, it was Atlas who held up the heavens (i.e. the sky, not the globe of the world). Atlas, "keeps the sky at bay, / The sack of black! It is everywhere, tight, tight!" What does night/blackness represent here? Who or what might Atlas represent in the life of the mother and/or the child?

5. Presumably, the five brass cannonballs at the feet of Atlas are another detail on the candlestick. What is the significance of the word "when" in the final line? (The final line makes me think of Nero playing the lyre while Rome burned!)

ARIEL

Many of the difficulties of this poem disappear when you know that Ariel was the name of Plath's horse and is Hebrew for 'God's Lion'.

1. Which lines in the first three verses clearly refer to riding a horse?

2. What time of the day is it and how do you know?

3. As she rides through the air what happens to the speaker as described in verses six and seven?

4. The speaker seems to change her physical state in verse eight. To what?

5. What is the "red Eye"? What happens to the speaker?

POPPIES IN OCTOBER

The unseasonal appearance of poppies so late in the year seems a staggering gift out of place with everything else.

1. Verse one contains two comparisons used to describe the redness of the poppies: one is beautiful and the other shocking. Explain them both.

2. In verses 2 and 3 the "sky" and the 'eyes' are too dead to have asked for or to appreciate such a gift. How is this made clear?

3. The final verse once again stresses the unlikely element of the poppies. How?

4. "O my God, what am I". This line seems to encapsulate the impact which the poppies have upon the speaker. Try to explain in your own words.

NICK AND THE CANDLESTICK

Written 29th October, 1962. Many of the apparent difficulties of this poem disappear when the dramatic situation is explained: the speaker, woken by the crying of her baby in the night, takes a candle to light her way to the baby's room. Notice the contrast between the mood and atmosphere of verses one to seven with the remainder of the poem.

1. Explain the opening *metaphor*, "I am a miner".

2. In what ways is the *metaphor* of the stalactites made so negative?

3. In what ways is the *metaphor* of the "Black bat airs" made so negative?

4. Can you explain the reference to "holy Joes"? (Think religion.)

5. The lines, "And the fish, the fish - / Christ!..." involves a rather bitter joke. Do you know why?

6. How is religion presented so negatively?

7. The recovery of the candle flame in verses seven and eight seems to be *symbolic*. Of what?

8. How does the description of the child establish its purity?

9. Examine the final verse very carefully. It includes two *images*. Explain each.

LETTER IN NOVEMBER

The speaker walks in her orchard, squelching through the wet grass, happy but conscious of the wounds of past experience. (The "wall of old corpses" refers to a graveyard close to the Devon cottage where she lived with Hughes. Thermopylae is a mountain pass where, in 480 BC, a Spartan army fought to the last man against a much larger Persian force.)

1. In verses 1 and 2, how does the speaker describe autumn and the on-set of winter?

2. What reasons does the speaker give for feeling "so stupidly happy"?

3. Can you explain the line, "O love, O celibate"?

4. Can you explain the lines, "The irreplaceable / Golds bleed and deepen, the mouths of Thermopylae"?

DEATH & Co.

The poem describes the two forms which dead takes: on the one hand there is the traditional figure of terror and on the other a rather attractive and seductive figure.

Verses 1 - 5

(The reference in line 4 is to the illustrations of the English poet William Blake in which figures always have bulging eyes; "their Ionian Death-gowns" compares the folds of the babies' shrouds with the flutings of columns in the Greek Ionian style.)

1. List the unattractive physical features which are associated with death in its traditional form.

2. In what ways does death make fun of the speaker?

3. On first impression, what makes death in its other form appear attractive?

4. How does the speaker make it clear that she has seen through this apparent attraction?

Verses 6 - 7

5. Why do the flowers created by the frost on windows and the glitter of a frozen drop of dew equally speak of death?

MARY'S SONG

Written 19th November, 1962. The main **motifs** of the poem are: the **image** of total destruction in a nuclear holocaust, the fears of the mother for her child, the necessity of sacrifice and regeneration after suffering. The **images** proceed through a series of thought-leaps. "Cicatrix": the scar tissue that forms on a wound during healing.

1. Who is the "Mary" of the title? How do you know?

2. Verse 1 is at once a domestic description of the Sunday lamb cooking in the oven and, **symbolically**, a reference to the death of Christ on the cross. Can you explain how this association is achieved?

3. What do you make of the line, "A window, holy gold"?

4. The idea of the fire which melts the fat (turning it the "precious" color of liquid gold), leads onto the idea of the fire which destroys. What specific historical examples are given?

5. In what sense do the victims of such inhuman destruction "not die"?

6. What important change in the voice of the poem occurs in line 13?

7. The gray birds bear the message of death from the past, but the last three verses make it clear that the speaker feels that she already inhabits a burnt, post-holocaust, world. How?

8. How does the final line of the poem, return the reader to the subject of the first line?

WINTER TREES

Written 29th November, 1962.

Verse 1

1. What painting technique is used to describe the visual impression of the trees seen in fog?

2. "Memories growing, ring on ring" is a complex *image*, though not a particularly difficult one. What do you make of it?

Verse 2

3. For what qualities does the speaker envy the trees?

Verse 3

(Leda in Greek mythology was raped by Zeus in the shape of a swan. A pieta is a statue or painting of the Virgin Mary embracing the dead body of Christ.)

4. In what obvious sense are the trees "full of wings"? How does this lead naturally to the *image* of Leda and the swan?

5. Does the speaker mean that the trees are pietas? If so, why?

6. What is it that the "chanting" of the ringdoves fails to ease?

SHEEP IN FOG

The foggy day leads to depressing thoughts of the limitations of life. The first line is a very precise description of how the fog abruptly cuts off the line of the hills. The poem ends with a vision of death with no promise of an afterlife. Plath frequently uses water as a *symbol* of death.

1. The only reference to sheep is in the title of the poem. Can you account for this?

2. Explain the *image* of the morning "blackening" like "a flower left out".

3. Why do you think that the "far fields" seem to threaten?

THE MUNICH MANNEQUINS

The poem was written 28th January 1963. It contains a chain of **images** of desolation, coldness, loneliness and silence. The **theme** is sterility and bareness **symbolized** by white and productivity **symbolized** by the menstrual flow of blood. A mannequin is a human-like doll used to model clothes in shop windows.

Lines 1 - 15

1. In what sense is the "loveliness" of the mannequins a sort of "perfection"?

2. The line, "Orange lollies on silver sticks" is a description of the mannequins. (Mannequins are normally kept stable by a metal stand – the "stick".) What is the effect of this description?

3. Why is the monthly flow of menstrual blood "The absolute sacrifice"? Why is it "to no purpose"?

4. Give your ideas of the meaning of the lines, "It means: no more idols but me, / Me and you."

Lines 16 - 27

5. These lines broaden the description to the life of Munich. What points does the poem seem to be making about that life? How?

6. How is the second half of the poem a continuation of the idea and mood of the first half?

WORDS

Written on 1st February, 1963

1. In verses 1 and 2, how is the power of words established? (Look in particular at the **images**.)

2. In verses 3 and 4, how is it made clear that words quickly lose their power?

3. Susan Bassnett writes of this poem, "There is no sense at all of conscious crafting, of searching for effect. Instead there is a sense of spontaneity, of a poet using all the power she has stored up unconsciously, a sense of release." Do you agree with this comment on the style of the poem?

EDGE

Written on 5th February, 1963, the same day Plath wrote "Balloons". These were the last poems she wrote before her death. The subject is a woman who has killed herself. The moon looks on. Line 4 refers to the Greek view of suicide which was that taking one's own life was not always blameworthy; there were situations in which suicide was the only honorable action which a person could take. Line 11 may refer to the habit in some cultures of leaving out a saucer of milk for the house snake, but it may also be significant that Plath put out milk for her children before killing herself.

Verses 1 - 4

1. Explain the meaning of the first line.

2. What contribution do the words "illusion" and "seem" make to the meaning of these verses?

Verses 5 - 8

3. Verses 5 and 6 indicate that the woman has killed her children. How is this meaning made? The killing is not, of course, literal. In what sense has the woman killed her children in killing herself?

4. Explain the *image* of roses in verses 7 and 8.

Verses 9 - 10

5. Why is it that the moon is correct to look down on this suicide dispassionately?

6. The final line seems to refer to the black clouds which the moon is wearing like mourning. What do you make of the line, "Staring from her hood of bone"?

7. What parts of the poet do you still find difficult to understand? Why?

A Sample Essay: Sylvia Plath's Sense of Place

Those of Plath's poems which have a particular setting are typically located in places which represent or epitomize the extreme edge of existence: the meeting point of life and death, or the border line between civilization and wild nature. That Plath uses these landscapes as **symbols** is clear from an analysis of the poems "Wuthering Heights" and "Finisterre".

"Wuthering Heights" is set on the wild Yorkshire moors, and carries the inevitable literary associations of Emily Bronte's novel of the same name. One notices first the precise observation of the landscape with its horizons which:

> ... only dissolve and dissolve
> ... as I step forward.

Anyone familiar with walking in hilly moorland will recognize this description of the way in which one horizon is replaced by a further horizon as the walker advances. Plath also describes the effect of the dominant winds in such high moorland, "the wind ... bending / Everything in one direction." Plath's **theme**, however, is the age-old conflict between natural forces and human life. The speaker feels herself to be out of place and at the mercy of the elements:

> The sky leans on me, me, the one upright
> Among all horizontals.

This is a place where 'there is no life higher than the grasstops," and so the sky presses down upon the speaker to reduce her to submission. As the sky presses her down, so the heather appears to tempt the speaker downwards:

> If I pay the roots of the heather
> Too close attention, they will invite me
> To whiten my bones among them.

There is deliberate **irony** in the word "invite," for behind its politeness is a destructive process which has won victories for centuries, for the process with threatens the speaker is the same as that which has destroyed the buildings whose ruins she finds:

> Hollow doorsteps go from grass to grass;
> Lintel and sill have unhinged themselves.

Here the word "hollow" implies a verdict on the human condition, and "unhinged" suggests a loss of sanity when faced with primal destructive forces. This landscape thus represents the brutal (and seductive) forces of death in opposition to the will to live which is represented by the speaker.

Only the sheep are at home in this landscape since they seem to be part of the weather rather than of life. Their dirty wool makes them look like clouds and they are, "Gray as the weather." They look on sardonically at the uneven battle between life and death which rages before them - a battle in which even the grass is battered by the wind so that it appears to be, "beating its head distractedly" because "Darkness terrifies it." The speaker's only retreat is into the valleys where human life does survive, though it is only "small change" compared to the forces of death which rule Wuthering Heights.

"Finisterre" is one of several Plath poems set on the shores of the ocean. In reading these poems it is important to remember that for Plath the sea represents death and the land life - but ***ambiguously***, since death often appears to be the more attractive alternative. "Finisterre" explores the contrast between the scene as it used to be when the sailors of the village had to dare the waters of "the Bay of the Dead" for a living, and the scene as it is now when everything has been adapted and falsified for the tourist. It is the former which interests Plath; the latter she merely despises. The life and death struggle was between "the land's end: the last fingers" and:

> ... the sea exploding
> With no bottom, or anything on the other side of it,

The power of the sea is suggested by the verb "exploding," whilst life seems to be hanging onto the cliffs weakly but desperately with "rheumatic" fingers. Those who lived there turned to their religion for protection, and a statue represents the devotion of the peasants to "Our Lady of the Shipwrecked," but ***ironically*** the statue which celebrates their faith shows its pointlessness, for:

> She does not hear what the sailor or the peasant is saying -
> She is in love with the beautiful formlessness of the sea.

The second line epitomizes the attitude of the speaker, but in the modern world, the power of the sea (its romance and its threat) appears to have been tamed. It is now simply exploited to provide:

> ... pretty trinkets ...
> Little shells made up into necklaces and toy ladies.

The "Black" sea has been replaced by:

> ... another place, tropical and blue,
> We have never been to.'

The speaker has no interest in this sea. It is as though once the threat of death has been removed, life itself becomes only trivial and silly, like the tourist trinkets. ***Symbolically***, Finisterre was one place where the close proximity with death gave life the desperate energy to want to prolong itself.

Literary terms activity

As you use each term in the study guide, fill in the definition of the term and include an example from the text to show how it is used.

The first definition is supplied. Find an example in the text to complete it.

Term: ambiguity, ambiguous

Definition: *when a statement is unclear in meaning- ambiguity may be deliberate or accidental*

Example:

****

Term: image, imagery

Definition:

Example:

****

Term: irony, ironic, ironically

Definition:

Example:

****

Term: metaphor, metaphorical

Definition:

Example:

****

Term: paradox, paradoxical

Definition:

Example:

****

Term: personified, personification

Definition:

Example:

****

Selected Poems by Sylvia Plath

Term: pun

Definition:

Example:

****

Term: simile

Definition:

Example:

****

Term: symbol, symbolic, symbolism, symbolizes

Definition:

Example:

****

Term: theme

Definition:

Example:

****

Literary terms

NOTE Not all of these terms may be relevant to this particular study guide

Adjective: part of speech- a word that describes a noun (e.g. the <u>thin</u> man)

Allegorical: a story in which the characters, their actions and the settings represent abstract ideas (often moral ideas) or historical/ political events.

Ambiguous, ambiguity: when a statement is unclear in meaning- ambiguity may be deliberate or accidental

Analogy: a comparison which treats two things as identical in one or more specified ways

Antagonist: an opposing character or force to the protagonist

Antithesis: the complete opposite of something

Authorial comment: when the writer addresses the reader directly (not to be confused with the narrator doing so.)

Chorus figure: a representative character who reflects on /interprets the action for the reader (like the Chorus in Greek drama)

Climax: the conflict to which the action has been building since the start of the play or story.

Colloquialism: the casual, informal mainly spoken language of ordinary people - often called" slang".

Comic hyperbole: deliberately inflated, extravagant language used for comic effect

Comic Inversion: reversing the normal order of things for comic effect

Connotation: the ideas, feelings and associations generated by a word or phrase

Couplet: two lines of poetry whether rhymed of unrhymed.

Dark comedy: comedy which has a serious implication

Dialogue: a conversation between two or more people in direct speech

Diction: the writer's choice of words in order to create a particular effect

Dramatic function or purpose: some characters and plot devices in plays are used by the author for specific purposes necessary to the action

Dramatic significance: importance of an act, speech, or character in the context of the play itself

Equivocation: saying something which is capable of two interpretations with the intention of misrepresenting the truth

Euphemism: a polite word for an ugly truth for example, a person is said to be sleeping when they are actually dead

Fallacy: a misconception resulting from incorrect reasoning

Foreshadow: a statement or action which gives the reader a hint of what is likely to happen later in the narrative

Form of speech: the register in which speech is written - the diction reflects the character

Frame narrative: a story within which the main narrative is placed

Genre: the type of literature into which a particular text falls (e.g. drama, poetry, novel)

Hubris: pride- in Greek tragedy it is the hero's belief that he can challenge the will of the gods.

Image, imagery: figurative language such as simile, metaphor, personification etc., or a description which conjures u a particularly vivid picture

Imply, implication: when the text suggests to the reader a meaning which it does not actually state

Infer, inference: the reader's act of going beyond what is stated in the text to draw conclusions

Irony, ironic: a form of humor which undercuts the apparent meaning of a statement

Conscious irony: irony used deliberately by a writer or character

Unconscious irony: a statement or action which has significance for the reader of which the character is unaware

Dramatic irony: when an action has an important significance that is obvious to the reader but not to one or more of the characters

Tragic irony: when a character says (or does) something which will have a serious, even fatal, consequence for him/ her. The audience is aware of the error, but the character is not.

Verbal irony: the conscious use of particular words which are appropriate to what is being said

Juxtaposition: literally putting two things side by side for purposes of comparison and/ or contrast

Literal: the surface level of a statement

Machiavellian: a person for whom the end justifies the means - a devious, manipulative, character whose only concern is his/ her own good

Malapropism: the unconscious misuse of language by a character so that key words are replaced by similar sounding words, which make no sense in the context in which they are used, the effect being unintentionally comic

Melodramatic: action and/or dialogue that is inflated or extravagant- frequently used for comic effect

Metaphor, metaphorical: the description of one thing by direct comparison with another (e.g. the coal-black night)

> *Extended metaphor: a comparison which is developed at length*

Microcosm: literally 'the world is little' - a situation which reflects truths about the world in general

Mood: the feelings and emotions contained in and/ or produced by a work of art (text, painting, music, etc.)

Motif: a frequently repeated idea, image or situation

Motivation: why a character acts as he/ she does- in modern literature motivation is seen as psychological

Narrates, narrator: the voice that the reader hears in the text

> *Frame narrative /story: a story within which the main story is told (e.g. "heart of darkness" by Conrad begins with five men on a boat in the Thames and then one of them tells the story of his experiences on the river Congo)*

Oxymoron: the juxtaposition of two terms normally thought of as opposite (e.g. the silent scream)

Parable: a story with a moral lesson (e.g. the Good Samaritan)

Paradox, paradoxical: a statement or situation which appears self-contradictory and therefore absurd

Pathos: is pity, or rather the ability of a text to make the audience or reader feel pity

Perspective: point of view from which a story, or an incident within a story, is told

Personified, personification: a simile or metaphor in which an inanimate object or abstract idea is described by comparison with a human

Plot: a chain of events linked by cause and effect

Prologue: an introduction which gives a lead-in to the main story

Protagonist: the character who initiates the action and is most likely to have the sympathy of the audience

Pun: a deliberate play on words where a particular word has two or more meanings both appropriate in some way to what is being said

Realism: a text that describes the action in a way that appears to reflect life

Rhetoric: the art of public speaking and more specifically the techniques which make speaking and writing effective

Rhetorical device: any use of language designed to make the expression of ideas more effective (e.g. repetition, imagery, alliteration, etc.)

Rhyming couplets: two consecutive lines of poetry ending in a full rhyme

Rhythm: literally the 'musical beat' of the words. In good writing, the rhythm of the words is clearly appropriate to what the words describe, so the rhythm is a part of the total meaning of the words

Role: means function- characters in plays (particularly minor characters) frequently have specific functions

Sarcasm: stronger than irony - it involves a deliberate attack on a person or idea with the intention of mocking

Setting: the environment in which the narrative (or part of the narrative) takes place

Simile: a description of one thing by explicit comparison with another (e.g. my love is like a red, red rose)

Extended simile: a comparison which is developed at length

Soliloquy: where a character in a play, normally alone on the stage, directly addresses the audience. By convention, a character is truthful in a soliloquy, though they may, of course be wrong or self-deceiving

Style: the way in which a writer chooses to express him/ herself. Style is a vital aspect of meaning since how something is expressed can crucially affect what is being written or spoken

Suspense: the building of tension in the reader

A Study Guide

Symbol, symbolic, symbolism, symbolize: a physical object which comes to represent an abstract idea (e.g. the sun may symbolize life)

Themes: important concepts, beliefs and ideas explored and presented in a text

Third person: third person singular is "he/ she/ it" and plural is "they" - authors often write novels in the third person

Tone: literally the sound of a text - How words sound (either in the mouth of an actor or the head of a reader) can crucially affect meaning

Tragic: King Richard III and Macbeth are both murderous tyrants, yet only Macbeth is a *tragic* figure. Why? Because Macbeth has the potential to be great, recognizes the error he has made and all that he has lost in making it, and dies bravely in a way that seems to accept the justice of the punishment.

Verse, structure of: Poets (unless they are writing free verse) choose to write within a set form - this may control line length and syllabic patterns, poem length, etc.

Selected Poems by Sylvia Plath

Classroom Use of Study Guide questions

Although there are both closed and open questions in the Study Guide, very few of them have simple, right or wrong answers. They are designed to encourage in-depth discussion, disagreement, and (eventually) consensus. Above all, they aim to encourage students to go to the text to support their conclusions and interpretations.

I am not so arrogant as to presume to tell teachers how they should use this resource. I used it in the following ways, each of which ensured that students were well prepared for class discussion and presentations.

1. Set a reading assignment for the class and tell everyone to be aware that the questions will be the focus of whole class discussion the next class.

2. Set a reading assignment for the class and allocate particular questions to sections of the class (e.g. if there are four questions, divide the class into four sections, etc.).

In class, form discussion groups containing one person who has prepared each question and allow time for feedback within the groups.

Have feedback to the whole class on each question by picking a group at random to present their answers and to follow up with class discussion.

3. Set a reading assignment for the class, but do not allocate questions.

In class, divide students into groups and allocate to each group one of the questions related to the reading assignment the answer to which they will have to present formally to the class.

Allow time for discussion and preparation.

4. Set a reading assignment for the class, but do not allocate questions.

In class, divide students into groups and allocate to each group one of the questions related to the reading assignment.

Allow time for discussion and preparation.

Now reconfigure the groups so that each group contains at least one person who has prepared each question and allow time for feedback within the groups.

5. Before starting to read the text, allocate specific questions to individuals or pairs. (It is best not to allocate all questions to allow for other approaches and variety. One in three questions or one in four seems about right.) Tell students that they will be leading the class discussion on their question. They will need to start with a brief presentation of the issues and then conduct a question and answer session. After this, they will be expected to present a brief review of the discussion.

6. Having finished the text, arrange the class into groups of 3, 4 or 5. Tell each group to select as many questions from the Study Guide as there are members of the group.

Each individual is responsible for drafting out a written answer to one question, and each answer should be a substantial paragraph.

To the Reader

Ray strives to make his products the best that they can be. If you have any comments or questions about this book *please* contact the author through his email: **moore.ray1@yahoo.com**

Visit his website at **http://www.raymooreauthor.com**

Also by Ray Moore: Most books are available from amazon.com as paperbacks and at most online eBook retailers.

Fiction:

The Lyle Thorne Mysteries: each book features five tales from the Golden Age of Detection:

Investigations of The Reverend Lyle Thorne
Further Investigations of The Reverend Lyle Thorne
Early Investigations of Lyle Thorne
Sanditon Investigations of The Reverend Lyle Thorne
Final Investigations of The Reverend Lyle Thorne

Non-fiction:

The **Critical Introduction series** is written for high school teachers and students and for college undergraduates. Each volume gives an in-depth analysis of a key text:

"The Stranger" by Albert Camus: A Critical Introduction (Revised Second Edition)
"The General Prologue" by Geoffrey Chaucer: A Critical Introduction
"Pride and Prejudice" by Jane Austen: A Critical Introduction
"The Great Gatsby" by F. Scott Fitzgerald: A Critical Introduction

The Text and Critical Introduction series differs from the Critical introduction series as these books contain the original text and in the case of the medieval texts an interlinear translation to aid the understanding of the text. The commentary allows the reader to develop a deeper understanding of the text and themes within the text.

"Sir Gawain and the Green Knight": Text and Critical Introduction
"The General Prologue" by Geoffrey Chaucer: Text and Critical Introduction
"The Wife of Bath's Prologue and Tale" by Geoffrey Chaucer: Text and Critical Introduction
"Heart of Darkness" by Joseph Conrad: Text and Critical Introduction
"The Sign of Four" by Sir Arthur Conan Doyle Text and Critical Introduction
"A Room with a View" By E.M. Forster: Text and Critical Introduction
"Oedipus Rex" by Sophocles: Text and Critical Introduction

Study guides available in print- listed alphabetically by author

* *denotes also available as an eBook*
"ME and EARL and the Dying GIRL" by Jesse Andrews: A Study Guide

Selected Poems by Sylvia Plath

"Wuthering Heights" by Emily Brontë: A Study Guide *

"Jane Eyre" by Charlotte Brontë: A Study Guide *

"The Myth of Sisyphus" and "The Stranger" by Albert Camus: Two Study Guides *

"The Meursault Investigation" by Kamel Daoud: A Study Guide

"Great Expectations" by Charles Dickens: A Study Guide *

"The Sign of Four" by Sir Arthur Conan Doyle: A Study Guide *

"A Room with a View" by E. M. Forster: A Study Guide

"Looking for Alaska" by John Green: A Study Guide

"Paper Towns" by John Green: A Study Guide

"Unbroken" by Laura Hillenbrand: A Study Guide

"The Kite Runner" by Khaled Hosseini: A Study Guide

"A Thousand Splendid Suns" by Khaled Hosseini: A Study Guide

"Go Set a Watchman" by Harper Lee: A Study Guide

"On the Road" by Jack Keruoac: A Study Guide

"The Secret Life of Bees" by Sue Monk Kidd: A Study Guide

"An Inspector Calls" by J.B. Priestley: A Study Guide

"The Catcher in the Rye" by J.D. Salinger: A Study Guide

"Macbeth" by William Shakespeare: A Study Guide *

"Othello" by William Shakespeare: A Study Guide *

"Antigone" by Sophocles: A Study Guide *

"Oedipus Rex" by Sophocles: A Study Guide

"Cannery Row" by John Steinbeck: A Study Guide

"East of Eden" by John Steinbeck: A Study Guide

"Of Mice and Men" by John Steinbeck: A Study Guide *

Study Guides available as e-books:

"Heart of Darkness" by Joseph Conrad: A Study Guide

"The Mill on the Floss" by George Eliot: A Study Guide

"Lord of the Flies" by William Golding: A Study Guide

"Catch-22" by Joseph Heller: A Study Guide

"Life of Pi" by Yann Martel: A Study Guide

"Nineteen Eighty-Four by George Orwell: A Study Guide

"Selected Poems" by Sylvia Plath: A Study Guide

"Henry IV Part 2" by William Shakespeare: A Study Guide

"Julius Caesar" by William Shakespeare: A Study Guide

"The Pearl" by John Steinbeck: A Study Guide

"Slaughterhouse-Five" by Kurt Vonnegut: A Study Guide

"The Bridge of San Luis Rey" by Thornton Wilder: A Study Guide

Teacher resources: Ray also publishes many more study guides and other resources for classroom use on the 'Teachers Pay Teachers' website: **http://www.teacherspayteachers.com/Store/Raymond-Moore**

Printed in Great Britain
by Amazon